500 REPORT CARD COMMENTS

A POINTER IN THE RIGHT DIRECTION FOR EDUCATORS

DR DHEERAJ MEHROTRA

Copyright © Dr Dheeraj Mehrotra
All Rights Reserved.

This book has been self-published with all reasonable efforts taken to make the material error-free by the author. No part of this book shall be used, reproduced in any manner whatsoever without written permission from the author, except in the case of brief quotations embodied in critical articles and reviews.

The Author of this book is solely responsible and liable for its content including but not limited to the views, representations, descriptions, statements, information, opinions and references ["Content"]. The Content of this book shall not constitute or be construed or deemed to reflect the opinion or expression of the Publisher or Editor. Neither the Publisher nor Editor endorse or approve the Content of this book or guarantee the reliability, accuracy or completeness of the Content published herein and do not make any representations or warranties of any kind, express or implied, including but not limited to the implied warranties of merchantability, fitness for a particular purpose. The Publisher and Editor shall not be liable whatsoever for any errors, omissions, whether such errors or omissions result from negligence, accident, or any other cause or claims for loss or damages of any kind, including without limitation, indirect or consequential loss or damage arising out of use, inability to use, or about the reliability, accuracy or sufficiency of the information contained in this book.

Made with ♥ on the Notion Press Platform
www.notionpress.com

Contents

Preface

Teaching itself extends well beyond the confines of just transmitting academic information. It is an art, a science, and a human endeavour that can move people to tears, mould the minds of the next generation, and sculpt the future. Feedback is a powerful instrument that can affirm, inspire, and drive others, and it plays an essential role in this delicate process. The book "500 Report Card Comments" is more than simply a collection of comments; instead, it embodies that input, which has been painstakingly crafted to represent the complexities and complexity of the student-teacher relationship.

As a result of my extensive teaching experience and lifelong interest in the field of education, I can empathise with the difficulties that classroom instructors encounter daily. Even while the remarks on a student's report card may appear like a relatively small portion of an educator's duties, they are critical in conveying information about a student's development, successes, difficulties, and potential for improvement. It is not enough to state how well a student has done; instead, providing constructive, practical and personalised feedback is necessary so that both kids and their parents understand it.

This book is intended to assist instructors from various backgrounds as a thorough guide, a ready reckoner. It doesn't matter whether you're just starting in this honourable profession or have been teaching for decades; these observations summarize the diverse range of feelings, successes, and difficulties a student may encounter throughout an academic year. Every remark has been painstakingly constructed, considering the variety of student characteristics, accomplishments, and difficulties. They may be used as a model, but the flexibility they provide is where most of their strength rests. The instructors are urged to make these remarks their own by personalising them, infusing them with unique insights, and making them their own. Feedback will never change in the education system, although educational procedures and approaches are continually refined and improved. It is the connection between teaching and learning, the medium instructors communicate with their pupils. This bridge has to be strengthened to make the feedback process more informative, productive, and uplifting. "500 Report Card Comments" is an effort to strengthen this bridge. You are about to go on a trip through the pages of this book. As you do so, I want you to come across the words that speak to your kid's experience, words that will inspire and drive them, and words that will, above all else, genuinely capture the spirit of their academic year. Teachers can use these comments to inspire and encourage students in their academic journey, emphasizing the importance of effort, growth, and determination.

With best regards,

www.authordheerajmehrotra.com

CHAPTER ONE

IMPORTANCE OF MOTIVATION TO STUDENTS

Students may benefit immensely from receiving positive feedback for a variety of reasons, including the following:

Positive conduct is easier to maintain when it is acknowledged and praised. When you acknowledge and praise a student's effort or behaviour, you reinforce that behaviour, increasing the likelihood that the student will continue to demonstrate that behaviour.

Boosts Confidence and Self-Esteem Receiving positive comments is one of the best ways to boost a student's self-esteem and confidence. Students are more inclined to take on new tasks and test the limits of their abilities when they have confidence in themselves.

Recognition of a student's efforts or accomplishments may be an effective method of fostering motivation in that kid. It sends the message to the student that their efforts are being seen and acknowledged, encouraging them to keep putting in their effort.

Encouraging a Pleasant Learning Setting An environment that encourages a pleasant learning experience may help students accomplish more and succeed in school. The development of mutual respect and the promotion of open communication are both fostered by the positive remarks that help to the formation of this environment.

Develops Resilience: Receiving positive comments may assist pupils in better coping with negative experiences. When someone is aware that they have strengths and have received praise in the past for those abilities, they can depend on those affirmations when they are confronted with problems.

Builds Trust Between Students and Instructors Positive remarks help students and instructors connect on a deeper level, strengthening the relationship between the two parties. When they feel their professors respect and understand them, students are more willing to approach them with their difficulties or seek help.

Motivates Students to Take Part in Class Discussions and Activities Students who are given positive comments are likelier to participate actively in class, express their thoughts, and participate in group work activities.

Learning That Is Tailored To Each Individual By praising certain parts of a student's work or conduct, instructors can better direct their pupils' attention to the subject matter that requires the most effort, facilitating more specialized and efficient learning.

A balanced perspective acknowledges that although providing students with helpful criticism is necessary, it is also crucial to draw attention to the positive aspects of the student's performance. This balance guarantees that pupils don't only concentrate on their shortcomings but also identify their strengths and build upon them rather than simply focusing on how they can improve their deficiencies.

Encourages a development attitude. Positive feedback, particularly remarks that praise an individual's work rather than their innate talent encourages a development attitude. Students are encouraged to regard problems as chances for progress and to comprehend that capabilities and intellect may be developed through effort when presented with this viewpoint.

To get to the heart of the matter, favourable remarks are more than just words of appreciation. They are instruments that, when utilized correctly, can mould the academic path, mental well-being, and general attitude of a student toward learning and problems in general.

CHAPTER TWO

500 Report Card Comments

Demonstrates a significant step forward in [the topic].

Maintains a level of performance that is commensurate with the grade level.

Demonstrates a strong command of the [subject's] fundamental ideas.

Although they struggle sometimes with challenging subjects, they continue to show determination.

Maintains a high standard of excellence in [the topic].

Contributes in a way that demonstrates thoughtfulness while participating in class discussions.

Has a positive attitude toward the [topic].

Demonstrates the ability to think critically.

Would benefit from more research being done on [the topic].

Pays attention and participates actively throughout classes.

Exhibits respect for one's coworkers and one's peers.

Requires constant reiteration of the rules of the classroom.

Interrupts other students in class regularly.

He is a delightful presence in the classroom.

Develop fruitful ties with one's contemporaries.

Participates in collaborative projects with success.

The inability to cooperate reasonably with others.

Demonstrates the attributes of a leader.

Demonstrates politeness and a refined demeanour.

Listening abilities need to be developed further.

Maintains a timely completion rate for tasks.

Organizational skills need to be improved.

Demonstrates initiative in the learning environment.

Tends to forget assignments.

Always arrive at class with the necessary materials.

Needs to be reminded of upcoming deadlines.

Exhibits diligence and perseverance in the face of adversity.

Gains can be had by taking regular breaks while working.

They are very careful in their written work.

Encouragement is required to keep working on the job at hand.

Always keen to take part in whatever is going on.

Could have a more active role if desired.

Frequently reluctant to talk about their opinions.

During presentations, he exhibits an air of self-assurance.

Learner with a positive attitude.

Gains that come from receiving specialized attention.

Functions effectively on its own.

Hesitates to seek assistance from others.

Like to work alone and in complete silence.

Reads at a level that is more advanced than their grade level.

Having trouble working with mathematical problems.

He has an avid interest in historical topics.

Additional help in the scientific realm is required.

Performs very well in creative writing activities.

Reading assignments are a challenge for the individual in terms of understanding.

Has an innate ability in the arts.

Has an excellent feel for the beat in the music lesson.

During physical education, demonstrates tremendous athletic ability and potential.

Demonstrates an in-depth familiarity with the principles related to [the topic].

Commentary on Attitude and Effort:

Always gives one's utmost effort.

Manifests a constructive and optimistic outlook.

Demands that one be motivated.

Puts pride in their job.

Demonstrates a passion for intellectual pursuits.

A lot of the time, he appears uninterested.

Displays tenacity despite being confronted with obstacles.

Is one who gives up easily.

Maintains a steady level of effort.

Exhibits a strong capacity for survival.

Commentary on our Strengths and Talents:

Has a lot of writing talent.

Is a master at finding solutions to complex problems.

Has a natural ability in the arts of sketching and painting.

Has a sharp eye for detail.

Has a natural talent for narrating stories.

Demonstrates a high level of analytical ability.

Exhibits a high level of originality in initiatives.

Possesses an excellent memory.

Performs well in hands-on activities.

Is capable of rational thought.

Potential Improvement Areas Comments:

Would improve with some more reading drills.

Handwriting has to be a primary focus.

Should improve on skills related to time management.

Could profit from the guidance of their peers.

Participation is an area that needs improvement.

Should seriously consider becoming a member of a study group.

Gains can be had by doing more mathematical practice.

Should put more effort into their presentations.

Participating in a reading group could be beneficial for you.

In terms of written language, more experience is required.

Feedback about the Whole:

It is a pleasure to teach.

Calls for help on an individual basis.

Would be better off with more difficult tasks.

Frequently necessitates a course correction.

Has a high level of internal drive.

Displays signs of maturity.

Advantages derived from being encouraged.

Demands that you keep a close eye on it at all times.

Has come a long way in a short amount of time.

Aspires to the highest possible standard.

Is becoming better at managing their time.

Skills in taking notes are something that needs to be improved.

Exceptional research talents are shown here.

The individual has difficulty with test-taking techniques.

Perhaps some further practice would be beneficial.

Consists in acquiring better-organising abilities.

Needs to pay attention to the specifics.

Clearly demonstrates progress in the [described ability].

[Particular ability] calls for further practice and attention.

Is making progress in the development of their skills.

Capacity for Adaptation and Flexibility Comments:

Easily adapts to new variations in the program.

When routines are interrupted, there are struggles.

Demonstrates flexibility in terms of learning approaches.

Is willing to experiment with different approaches.

Can be averse to the adoption of novel concepts.

Exhibits versatility while working in a collaborative environment.

Demonstrates adaptability in both thinking and the resolution of problems.

Has difficulty making the transitions between different pursuits.

Exhibits a resilient demeanour when placed in unexpected settings.

Could benefit from increasing their level of adaptability via practice.

Cooperation and Working Together in Teams Comments:

Is a member of the team.

Struggles while working in a group setting.

Exhibits leadership in the context of a group.

Frequently acts as the focal point of group conversations.

Is a member of the team that assists.

Gains from receiving instruction on effective teamwork techniques.

Participates attentively in group activities by listening.

Can find it difficult to divide up tasks between themselves.

Constantly stands ready to provide a hand to their comrades.

Could improve their ability to communicate with one another.

Provides a straightforward expression of concepts.

Verbal expressiveness is an area that needs improvement.

Clearly express themselves through their writing.

They have difficulty expressing their views in words.

Demonstrates the ability to engage in active listening.

Interrupts other people often.

Capable of articulating complicated ideas and thoughts.

Need assistance in the development of better communication skills.

Has a very extensive vocabulary.

Participating in a speaking club could be beneficial for you.

Observations Made With Curiosity and Enthusiasm:

Always willing to gain knowledge in new areas.

Could have asked a more significant number of questions in class.

Has a strong interest in [a particular topic].

Demonstrates a passion for intellectual pursuits.

Can, at times, be reluctant to investigate novel subject matter.

Is never lacking in curiosity.

Can reap the benefits of channelling passion in a productive direction.

Exhibits enthusiasm for tasks that need hands-on participation.

Always look for opportunities to learn more.

Manifests a healthy dose of inquisitiveness.

Has an internal drive or motivation.

It is often necessary to seek inspiration from other sources.

Establishes and achieves one's objectives.

It might be challenging to maintain one's motivation in [topic].

Exhibits determination in all areas of responsibility.

Maintains a positive attitude in the face of adversity.

May profit by establishing objectives for the near future.

Has a strong desire to achieve success.

Could require some reinforcement to maintain their motivation.

Has a strong interest in their personal development.

Demonstrates an exceptional ability to solve problems.

Can, at times, get stalled when confronted with hurdles.

Demonstrates a critical thinking approach to complex challenges.

Would be helped by receiving extra techniques for problem-solving.

Adopts a systematic way of doing things.

Demonstrates the ability to think beyond the box.

Might benefit from practising critical thinking more with activities.

Performs analyses of challenges from a variety of perspectives.

Able to breeze through activities requiring problem-solving.

Demonstrates the ability to think.

Commentaries on Creativity and Innovation:

Imagination is strong in this person.

Generates one's unique concepts and thoughts.

Exhibits creative thinking in the work that they do.

Could benefit from pursuing their artistic interests in more ways.

Considers new possibilities.

Performs well in creative tasks.

Is unafraid to think in a non-traditional way.

Can, at times, depend on tried-and-true methods to solve problems.

Enjoys experimenting with a wide variety of artistic media.

Could focus on increasing the bounds of artistic expression.

Development of Emotional and Social Skills Remarks:

Exhibits compassion for one's peers.

Displays a high level of emotional intelligence.

Struggles to keep their emotions in check.

Has developed enduring relationships with others.

Can sometimes pull away from social interaction.

Exhibits consistently high levels of compassion.

They have a hard time comprehending the feelings of their peers.

Is thoughtful and sensitive to others' needs.

Can, at times, display very high levels of emotion.

Put your efforts towards cultivating healthy connections with others.

Commentary on Feedback and a Growth Mindset:

Positively accepts comments as given.

When getting feedback, may take a defensive stance.

Manifests characteristics of a development mentality.

Sometimes, it exhibits a mentality that is established in its ways.

Is always seeking new methods to become better.

Demonstrates a capacity for perseverance in the face of adversity.

Responds well to constructive criticism.

Struggles to accept responsibility for their faults.

Takes in input and uses it to inform improved efforts.

I'm thrilled with how far we've come this semester!

Inspire them to keep up their efforts at home.

I am looking forward to seeing much more progress in this area.

Maintain the high quality of your work!

It would be strengthened with the use of consistent editing.

Always a pleasure to have in the classroom.

Fostering a more engaged and active involvement.

Has a promise but fails to capitalize on it ultimately.

Maintain your sense of wonder, and never stop adventuring!

Excellent work! Excited about the trip that lies in wait.

Paying Attention and Being Concentrated Remarks:

During tasks, demonstrates a high level of attentiveness.

Capable of maintaining focus for lengthy amounts of time.

The advantages of taking regular breaks while working.

Demonstrates a capacity to ignore irrelevant stimuli and focus on the task.

Can get the benefits of techniques that improve attention.

Demonstrates an increase in focus during the term.

Maintaining concentration during group conversations might be difficult for them.

Demonstrates extreme care and attention to detail.

Frequently hurriedly completes projects without giving them enough attention.

Maintains the order of the items and the working space.

Frequently has difficulty locating the appropriate supplies.

Makes effective plans and use of one's time.

Would profit enormously from the use of a planner or checklist.

Maintains a consistent record of meeting deadlines.

Tends to put off working on more significant jobs.

During project work, demonstrates a high level of organisational abilities.

Keeps the binder and workbook in a clean and organized state.

During timed tasks, they have difficulty maintaining a consistent pace.

Comments on Participation and Being Engaged in the Classroom:

Takes an active role in the talks that take place.

They can be shy in expressing their ideas.

Frequently displays initiative in the activities of the classroom.

Maintains attentive listening even while not actively taking part in the conversation.

They can gain by being more engaged throughout their studies.

During interactive sessions, demonstrates a high level of excitement.

Sometimes, they talk before their turn has been called.

They would be helped by raising their hand more often.

They are more of a quiet observer but need to speak out more.

Participates thoughtfully and actively in group conversations.

Always courteous to both one's classmates and one's professors.

Sometimes, he has trouble maintaining appropriate behaviour in the classroom.

Demonstrates patience and an ability to comprehend.

Has been known to interrupt other people on occasion.

Takes responsibility for the upkeep of school property.

They should be reminded to show respect for personal boundaries more often.

Serves as an excellent example for other students in the class.

Has bouts of impulsivity and is actively attempting to improve their self-control.

Addresses disputes in a level-headed and mature manner.

They could benefit from learning techniques to deal with their frustration.

Demonstrates a high degree of autonomy in the tasks.

Seek affirmation somewhat often; they should trust their judgment more.

Accepts personal responsibility for their education.

Can place an unhealthy amount of reliance on the support of peers.

It learns from its errors and uses that knowledge to improve itself.

They have difficulty reaching out for assistance when they are stranded.

Manifests a sense of self-confidence in one's talents.

The person has to increase their confidence in their own job.

Takes the initiative to help out other people often.

Should get into the habit of more successfully arguing for one's own demands.

Is always well-prepared for every lesson.

Demonstrates a passion for intellectual pursuits.

Maintains an optimistic attitude in the face of adversity.

Demonstrates significant growth in [particular sector].

Strives for excellence while acknowledging that it's OK to make errors.

Contributes an interesting new angle to the conversation.

Maintains a close engagement with the subject matter.

Can get the benefits of more practice as well as review.

Always courteous and a joy to work within the classroom.

Prepare yourself for even more successful outcomes in the subsequent term!

Your enthusiasm for learning shines brightly in class.

I'm genuinely impressed with your perseverance this term.

Keep harnessing that positive energy; it's truly infectious!

Your dedication to self-improvement is commendable.

Your improvement in [subject] demonstrates your commitment.

You've shown immense growth in tackling challenges head-on.

Your resilience in tough times is truly inspirational.

It's heartening to see you embrace feedback constructively.

Your zest for knowledge sets a benchmark.

You've pushed your boundaries this term.

You have an admirable 'never give up' attitude.

Your hard work and dedication are evident in your projects.

You're discovering your potential, and it's wonderful to witness.

The sky's the limit for you; keep aiming high.

I admire your ability to bounce back from setbacks.

Your collaborative spirit uplifts the entire class.

Your journey of self-discovery is truly commendable.

Each day, you come closer to realizing your potential.

Your consistent effort is a testament to your dedication.

I can see the spark of a lifelong learner in you.

Your positive outlook is a refreshing change.

Your dedication to mastering [specific skill] has paid off.

You believe in the power of hard work.

You're laying a strong foundation for future success.

Your hunger for knowledge is truly commendable.

I love your ability to turn challenges into opportunities.

The progress you've made this year is commendable.

Your willingness to take feedback is a strength.

Your commitment to your goals is evident.

I'm proud to see you taking charge of your learning.

Every challenge you face is an opportunity in disguise, and you understand that.

Your journey this year speaks volumes about your character.

I've noticed your proactive nature, and it's impressive.

Your confidence in approaching new challenges is motivating.

I love how you celebrate results and the effort you put in.

Your work reflects your dedication to excellence.

I can see a future leader in you. Keep shining!

Embracing challenges with an open heart has been your strength.

I'm inspired by your ability to handle pressure with grace.

Your ability to remain consistent is admirable.

Keep channelling your energy positively; you're on the right track.

Your curiosity is a gateway to endless possibilities.

I value your commitment to personal and academic growth.

Your determination is your biggest asset.

Every assignment showcases your passion and dedication.

The progress in [subject] is a reflection of your hard work.

With your determination, there's nothing you can't achieve.

Your passion for learning is contagious.

You've truly outdone yourself this term.

Your approach to problem-solving is innovative.

I've noticed your unwavering focus, and it's commendable.

The patience you exhibit while learning is a true strength.

Your proactive nature has been a game-changer this term.

Keep up the hard work, and great things await.

Your attitude towards challenges is commendable.

You're learning the importance of persistence, and it's showing.

Your journey this term showcases your indomitable spirit.

Continue to chase excellence, and success will follow.

Your quest for knowledge is inspiring.

The effort you put into your assignments shines through.

You've made notable improvements in areas you've focused on.

The diligence you've shown is a mark of your character.

Your growth mindset sets you apart.

Your commitment to growth and learning is palpable.

I admire your ability to keep pushing your limits.

It's wonderful to see you believing in yourself.

Your thirst for knowledge is your biggest strength.

Each assignment reflects your deepening understanding.

You've showcased true grit and determination this term.

Your open-minded approach to feedback is commendable.

Your journey is a testament to your resilience.

Continue embracing challenges; they shape champions.

Your passion for [subject] is evident in your work.

Your attitude towards learning lights up the classroom.

I value your consistent efforts and determination.

You're cultivating habits that will ensure future success.

Your perseverance will open doors to numerous opportunities.

I'm proud of the maturity you've displayed this term.

Every task you undertake reflects your commitment.

Your proactive approach to learning is impressive.

Keep that spark alive; your potential is limitless.

I'm excited to see where your dedication takes you.

Your hard work and persistence are undeniable.

Your growth this term has been nothing short of remarkable.

Your tenacity will surely lead you to great success.

I'm inspired by your unwavering commitment to your goals.

Your journey of growth and self-improvement is commendable.

Keep nurturing your curiosity; it's your superpower.

Your effort and dedication are clear indicators of future success.

Your can-do attitude is an inspiration to us all.

Your dedication to improving every day is evident.

Challenges are stepping stones, and you're climbing them admirably.

Your work showcases your dedication to mastering the subject.

It's heartening to see you take ownership of your learning.

You've turned challenges into learning opportunities.

Your commitment to understanding rather than rote learning is impressive.

Every challenge faced is a lesson learned, and you understand that.

Your efforts this term are a clear indicator of your potential.

The resilience you've showcased this term is exemplary.

Your dedication is shaping you into an exceptional learner.

You've harnessed the power of dedication beautifully this term.

You're learning to challenge yourself in exciting ways.

Your tenacity in confronting difficult subjects is commendable.

The way you handle feedback reflects your maturity and understanding.

Every task you've tackled speaks volumes of your determination.

You're emerging as a dedicated and self-motivated learner.

Your quest for perfection in your assignments is truly impressive.

Your inquisitive nature will lead you to greater discoveries.

You've demonstrated a wonderful can-do spirit this term.

It's heartening to see you stretch your boundaries.

Your proactive approach to understanding complex topics is admirable.

Your dedication to the subject is evident in each assignment.

I applaud your growth mindset and urge you to keep it alive.

With every challenge, you rise stronger and more determined.

I see a student determined to make the most of every learning opportunity.

Your dedication to self-growth shines through in your work.

The way you challenge yourself is truly inspiring.

I've noticed your efforts in taking constructive criticism in stride.

Your dedication to expanding your horizons is truly commendable.

Your consistent efforts are the hallmark of a true learner.

The classroom lights up with your enthusiasm and curiosity.

Your courage in facing academic challenges is remarkable.

Every piece of your work showcases the efforts behind it.

Your attitude towards embracing new learning methods is impressive.

I value your ability to reflect on and learn from mistakes.

Your work is a testament to the power of dedication and perseverance.

Your growth trajectory this term has been impressive.

Your commitment to the subject shines through in your assignments.

Maintain your enthusiasm for taking on new tasks.

You're on a path that will make you an excellent student.

Your tenacity and resolve have inspired many people.

You place equal value on getting there as you do on arriving there.

It's inspiring to see how patiently you've worked to learn something new.

I'm pleased with where you've been and what your future holds.

The progress you've made in [insert topic here] is quite encouraging.

You have shown tremendous resilience in the face of adversity.

You're becoming better with every move you make.

Your persistent effort shows how much you value comprehension.

You have been an inspiration to everyone around you this semester.

Keep tapping into the strength of your convictions; they are taking you far.

Your work demonstrates a serious interest in education.

You've implemented everyone's suggestions.

Your success is a tribute to your dedication and perseverance.

I have no doubt that, with your dedication, you will reach new heights.

It's inspiring to see you take on complex issues head-on.

Putting in work shows your progress with each submission.

Your growth this semester is impressive.

Your infectious zeal for personal growth makes me want to challenge myself more.

It's clear that you put in a lot of effort to improve your abilities.

It is inspiring to see how far you've come from average performance to greatness.

I really respect your dedication to producing high-quality results.

The ability to reflect on and improve upon past errors is a notable quality of yours.

Your enthusiasm for [topic] is inspiring.

You're doing well at overcoming each new obstacle you encounter.

You stand out because of how hard you work to better yourself.

You have an amazing capacity to prioritize your studies and see them through to completion.

I like your commitment and motivation in class.

The progress you've made this semester is impressive.

You have a remarkable capacity for growth and change.

Your relentless pursuit of quality never ceases to astound me.

Your work this semester is a great example of your ability.

I see a pupil who is willing to take on any obstacle.

Seeing how much you've improved in the classroom is motivating.

It's inspiring to see you so dedicated to learning and comprehension.

You consistently demonstrate that with hard work and perseverance, every goal is attainable.

You have shown thorough comprehension in all of your projects and homework.

It's impressive that you can take suggestions and make real changes.

Your diligence and perseverance are much

appreciated.

Your genuine interest in the topic shines through in all of your work.

Your relentless pursuit of excellence is evident in everything that you do.

I think you're doing well and want you to keep pushing the envelope.

Your willingness to face adversity head-on is an inspiration.

I like the effort and professionalism you put into your homework.

You have clearly established and met lofty goals for yourself.

Your ambition to better yourself day after day is inspiring.

Your work shows that you are committed to learning as well as completing homework.

You appear to have a firm grasp on the concept that every difficulty represents a

potential gain.

Your hard work is having a profound effect on your education.

Your diligence and dedication to improving in [topic] have been remarkable.

Your progress this semester has been very amazing to see.

Your tasks always impress me with their high standard of quality and thoughtfulness.

Your dedication to quality shines through in all of your work.

It's inspiring to see how you've used adversity to propel yourself forward.

Your commitment to challenging yourself is palpable.

I respect your enthusiasm for taking on any problem.

Your dedication to personal development speaks volumes about who you are as a person.

You have repeatedly shown that persistence and commitment pay off.

The depth and precision of your expertise is on display in your work.

I see an ambitious student with each project.

Your diligence and commitment are an example to others.

You have shown both comprehension and dedication in your assignments.

If you keep at it, you will succeed beyond your wildest dreams.

I like the wealth of knowledge you bring to the table in class.

Your enthusiasm for education shines through in all of your work.

Your dedication to succeeding is inspiring.

Your hard work and commitment to your tasks are commendable.

You are setting yourself up for future success with your development mentality.

Your enthusiasm and hard work show in everything you do.

Your dedication to achieving academic success is motivating.

You have the makings of a serious student; keep up the good work!

Your unflinching commitment to your academics is quite admirable.

Your dedication to learning challenging material is admirable.

Your capacity to continually push oneself is inspiring.

Your progression from hard work to achievement is reflected in every submission.

I know you will succeed because of your determination.

Your enthusiasm and dedication have been crucial to your accomplishments.

Your commitment to detail and thoroughness in your work is admirable.

You have repeatedly shown the value of dedication and concentration.

It's inspiring to see how seriously you're taking your studies.

Your sincerity shines through in all of your work.

With your dedication and perseverance, you will undoubtedly succeed.

Your willingness to challenge yourself is on full display in every task you turn in.

Your dedication and enthusiasm shine through in your finished product.

Your projects always show how motivated you are and how much you love learning.

It's inspiring to see your hard work pay off in the form of improved performance.

You've overcome every obstacle by showing that sheer will can do anything.

The secret to your success in school is the time and effort you put in every day.

You have shown amazing tenacity and commitment.

Every day that goes by, your commitment stands out more and more.

You've made some remarkable progress this semester.

Your tireless enthusiasm and commitment shine through in every one of your finished projects.

You're making wonderful academic progress thanks to your determination.

You seem to have mastered the skill of using

criticism as motivation to improve.

Seeing you reach your full potential is quite satisfying.

You're not only acquiring knowledge; you're developing the resilience and will to succeed in the real world.

You consistently exhibit the hallmarks of effort and enthusiasm in your work.

You're quite good at diving right into difficult situations.

The level of detail in your assignments is consistently impressive.

It's inspiring to see someone so focused on their academic goals.

Your efforts to exceed expectations have been inspiring.

You stand out due to your dedication to quality.

Your dedication to improvement is on full display in each of your projects.

Your toughness and resolve have been game-changing qualities this semester.

Your positive outlook is evidence of your resilience and perseverance.

You've shown remarkable development in response to each obstacle.

You have used all suggestions for improvement and made great strides.

About The Author

Dheeraj Mehrotra, MS, MPhil, PhD (Education Management)., a white and a yellow belt in SIX SIGMA, a Certified NLP Business Diploma holder, is an Educational Innovator, Author, with expertise in Six Sigma In Education, Academic Audits, Neuro-Linguistic Programming (NLP), Total Quality Management In Education, an Experiential Educator, a CBSE Resource towards School Assessment (SQAA), CCE, JIT, Five S, and KAIZEN. He has authored over 100 books on topics which include Computer Science, AI, Digital Body Language, NLP, Quality Circles, School Management, Classroom Effectiveness and Safety and Security in schools. A former Principal at De Indian Public School, New Delhi, (INDIA), NPS International School, Guwahati, and Education Officer at GEMS, Gurgaon, with ample teaching experience of over Two Decades, he is a certified Trainer for Quality Circles/ TQM in Education and QCI Standards for School Accreditation/ School Audits and Management. He has also been honoured with the President of India's National Teacher Award in 2006 and the Best Science Teacher State Award (By the Ministry of Science and Technology, State of UP), Innovation in Education for his inception of Six Sigma In Education by Education Watch, New Delhi and Education World- Best Teacher Award, BOLT Learner Teacher Award by Air India, 'Innovation in Education Award 2016' by Higher Education Forum (HEF), Gujarat Chapter, among others. He has developed over 150 FREE EDUCATIONAL MOBILE Apps for the Google Play Store exclusively for Teachers, Students, and Parents. This work has been recognised by the LIMCA

BOOK OF RECORDS & INDIA BOOK OF RECORDS as the only Indian to draw that feast. Dr Mehrotra is a PRINCIPAL at KUNWARS GLOBAL SCHOOL, Lucknow, in India. He has conducted over 1000 workshops globally on "Excellence In Education" integrated with Total Quality Management and Six Sigma, Technology Integration in Education (TIE), Developing towards being ROCKSTAR TEACHERS, including Cyberspace, Cyber Security, Classroom Management, School Leadership & Management, and Innovative teaching within classrooms via Mind Maps, NLP and Experiential Learning in Academics. He is an active TEDx speaker and can be viewed on the YouTube TEDx channel. As a premium UDEMY Instructor, he has developed over 450 courses and caters to over 8 Lakh students from 180 countries. He can be visited at www.authordheerajmehrotra.com

Books By The Same Author

www.ingramcontent.com/pod-product-compliance
Lightning Source LLC
LaVergne TN
LVHW021158160826
845679LV00024B/2156

* 9 7 9 8 8 9 1 3 3 5 5 0 9 *